THE ADVENTURE ZONE

Murder on the Rockport Limited!

Based on the podcast by

Griffin McElroy   Clint McElroy

Travis McElroy   Justin McElroy

Adaptation by

Clint McElroy   Carey Pietsch

Art by

Carey Pietsch

:01

First Second

New York

:01

First Second

Text copyright © 2019 by Clint McElroy, Griffin McElroy, Justin McElroy, Travis McElroy
Illustrations copyright © 2019 by Carey Pietsch
Letterer: Tess Stone

Flatters: Megan Brennan, Rachael Cohen, Cassandra Tassoni
Bulletin Board Photo Copyright © 2019 by Megan Brennan and Lisa Aurigemma
Fan Art Gallery Copyright © 2019 by (respectively):
Jay Pirfano
My Murphy
Gene Monteith McKechnie
Galogenida
Jeinu
Starlia Prichard
Pola Kowalewska
Haveafreakday
Nicky Beaton
Phoebe Ayscough
Karoline Stjernfelt
Devon Pasternak

Published by First Second
First Second is an imprint of Roaring Brook Press,
a division of Holtzbrinck Publishing Holdings Limited Partnership
120 Broadway, New York, NY 10271

Don't miss your next favorite book from First Second!
For the latest updates go to firstsecondnewsletter.com and sign up for our newsletter.

Library of Congress Control Number: 2018953551

ISBN: 978-1-250-15371-5 (Paperback)
ISBN: 978-1-250-22928-1 (Hardcover)
ISBN: 978-1-250-23436-0 (B&N Edition)
ISBN: 978-1-250-24004-0 (Indigo Edition)
ISBN: 978-1-250-25368-2 (BAM Edition)

Our books may be purchased in bulk for promotional, educational, or business use.
Please contact your local bookseller or the Macmillan Corporate and Premium Sales Department
at (800) 221-7945 ext. 5442 or by email at MacmillanSpecialMarkets@macmillan.com.

First edition, 2019
Edited by Calista Brill and Alison Wilgus
Book design by Andrew Arnold and Molly Johanson
Printed in the United States of America

Penciled with a 2B pencil-style tool in Procreate. Inked with a brush-style
digital nib in Clip Studio Paint and colored digitally in Photoshop.

Paperback: 10 9 8 7 6 5 4 3 2 1
Hardcover: 10 9 8 7 6 5 4 3 2 1

Chapter 1

MAGNUS BURNSIDES...

MERLE HIGHCHURCH...

TAAKO...

THE BUREAU OF BALANCE IS A VOLUNTEER ORGANIZATION.

I WON'T FORCE YOU TO JOIN.

BUT IF YOU DO, YOU'LL BECOME PART OF SOMETHING GRAND...

SOMETHING...

IMPORTANT.

THE WORK WE DO HERE IS FRAUGHT WITH PERIL.

I CAN'T PROMISE IT WILL BE EASY.

BUT I KNOW YOU ARE EQUAL TO THE TASK.

DAVENPORT!

DAVENPOOORT!

DAVENPORT
Race Davenport
Class Davenport
+PROFICIENCIES+
→ Davenport
→ Davenport
→ Davenport

THIS IS THE PART WHERE YOU HAND OVER THE GAUNTLET.

DON'T YOU MEAN "GAUNTLET OVER THE HAND"?

YOU KNOW... BECAUSE...IT'S LIKE...A GLOVE... AND...

!!!

??

WORKS FOR ME!

DUNK

IT'S GETTING ON MY LAST NERVE.

WHAT WE DO WOULD...NOT BE POSSIBLE WITHOUT THE VOIDFISH.

THE WAR, CALAMITY, AND TURMOIL YOU CAN NOW REMEMBER WAS A DIRECT RESULT OF DANGEROUS MAGICAL ARTIFACTS.

WHEN THESE ITEMS WERE CRAFTED AND WORD OF THEIR POWER SPREAD, EVERYONE WANTED THEM.

EVERY KINGDOM IN THE LAND, EVERY POLITICAL ORGANIZATION, MERCENARY GUILD, RELIGIOUS COMMUNITY...

THEY ALL MOUNTED EFFORTS TO CLAIM THE ARTIFACTS FOR THEIR OWN.

THAT LED TO A WAR THE LIKES OF WHICH THIS WORLD HAD NEVER SEEN.

AND THE ONLY WAY TO END THAT WAR...

...WAS TO MAKE EVERYONE FORGET THE ARTIFACTS EXISTED.

YOU SEE, OUR ORGANIZATION IS MADE UP OF THREE DIVISIONS.

THE FIRST GATHERS INFORMATION ON THE ARTIFACTS. THEY ARE KNOWN AS THE SEEKERS.

THE NEXT—

I KNOW! I KNOW! THEY'RE CALLED THE BEATERS!

AND THEN THE KEEPERS!

AND THE ONES WHO GRAB THE SNITCH! THE SNITCH-GRABBERS!

NO...THE RECLAIMERS.

THE SEEKERS ARE NOT PERMITTED TO COLLECT THE ARTIFACTS. THE RECLAIMERS ARE.

THAT'S THE JOB I'M OFFERING YOU.

DO WE GET A LICENSE TO KILL?

I DON'T—

HOW ABOUT A LICENSE TO CHILL?

THAT BRINGS US TO THE THIRD SECTION: THE REGULATORS.

ANYONE WHO USES INFORMATION GATHERED ABOUT THE ARTIFACTS FOR THEIR OWN WHIM, OR WHO WIELDS AN ARTIFACT, EVEN ONCE...

...WILL BE HUNTED DOWN AND PROPERLY DEALT WITH BY THE REGULATORS.

YOU'VE ALREADY MET OUR BEST REGULATOR...

...KILLIAN.

WHO?

FRIEND KILLIAN!

I REMEMBER YOU FROM THE FIRST BOOK!

KILLIAN

RACE — ORC
CLASS — WARRIOR
+ PROFICIENCIES +
→ Crossbow Wielding
→ Crisis management
→ Being patient with idiots

PLEASE, MAGNUS, MERLE, TAAKO—

JOIN US.

THE VERY EXISTENCE OF EVERYTHING WE KNOW AND LOVE MAY HANG IN THE BALANCE.

IS THERE DENTAL?

UH... YES?

COOL.

WE'RE IN.

13

GENTLEMEN, YOU ARE HEREBY ACCEPTED AS FULLY FLEDGED MEMBERS OF OUR ORDER.

AND WE ARE PROUD TO PRESENT YOU WITH THESE:

DAVENPORT!!

BRACERS OF BALANCE.

BRACERS of BALANCE
* FUNCTION *
→ Travel globe summoning
→ Oddly, helps carpal tunnel

YOU PEOPLE ARE REALLY INTO ALLITERATION.

THESE HAVE BEEN TAILOR-MADE FOR EACH OF YOU, AND ONCE YOU PUT THEM ON, THEY CAN NEVER BE REMOVED.

I'M WORRIED ABOUT "BRACER STINK." WHAT'S THE POLICY ON THAT? IS THERE SOME KIND OF DETERGENT?

UHHH... EACH INITIATE IS ISSUED A SPECIAL BRUSH...

...SO YOU CAN JUST...GET RIGHT IN THERE AND DO SOME... GROUTING.

GROSS, WHO WOULD EVER—

KLICK!

IT MEANS SO MUCH THAT YOU SHOWED UP TO JOIN IN WELCOMING US TO THE CLUB!

MY PRESENCE HERE IS MORE SYMBOLIC, REALLY.

A REGULATOR IS ALWAYS ON HAND WHEN A RECLAIMER JOINS. IT'S OUR WAY OF SAYING:

"I NOW KNOW YOUR FACE. THAT'LL MAKE IT EASIER TO HUNT YOU DOWN."

OH.

KIND OF AN AGGRESSIVE WORKPLACE ENVIRONMENT YOU GOT HERE.

KLIKK!

SO THAT'S IT? JUST ONE CRUMMY BRACER?

WHERE'S THE COOL WEAPONS AND MAGIC DUDS?

YEAH, WE WERE THINKING WE'D GET MORE THAN THAT...

YOU WILL TAKE THESE THREE TOKENS TO OUR ARTIFICER. HE WILL PROVIDE YOU WITH ADDITIONAL ITEMS.

I HOPE I GET A DOG!

THERE ARE NO DOGS—

—ON THE MOON!

IT'S FOR THEIR OWN GOOD. WE WORRY THAT THEY'LL JUST RUN OFF THE EDGE CHASING A STICK OR SOMETHING.

AND LET'S NOT FORGET—

FINALLY! IS IT GOING TO BE A CHECK? CASH? PROMISSORY NOTE?

OH, GOOD. A FANTASY TRAPPER KEEPER.

THAT WILL GUIDE YOU AS YOU GET TO KNOW THE MOON BASE...

...YOUR NEW HOME.

SURE, SURE.

I'M SEEING MAPS. ROOM SERVICE MENU. LAYOUT OF OUR ROOM—

...WAIT!

"ROOM"?! *SINGULAR?!*

I HAVE TO SHARE WITH THESE GUYS??

BUNKIES!!!!

LOOKS LIKE WE HAVE TO SEE "LEON THE ARTIFICER" FIRST.

ANOTHER DAMNED DOME.

ARCHITECTURALLY SPEAKING, IT'S REALLY NOT THE BEST USE OF SPACE.

WELCOME!

I AM LEON THE ARTIFICER!

AND THIS IS MY—

LEON
RACE Gnome
CLASS Artificer
PROFICIENCIES
→ Artificing
→ Frustration
→ Vending Machine
Expertise

I AM REALLY JONESING FOR A GUMBALL!

NO, IT'S—

A GASHAPON MACHINE!

NO. THIS IS MY—

VENDING MACHINE FROM SHENMUE!

NO—

FINE...

IT'S A BIG GASHAPON MACHINE FULL OF MAGICAL ITEMS.

ISN'T THE WHOLE POINT OF THIS ORGANIZATION TO KEEP PEOPLE FROM GETTING THEIR HANDS ON THIS KIND OF THING?

YES, IT'S TRUE THAT IT'S AGAINST THE STRICTURES OF OUR ORDER TO SPECIFICALLY GIVE OUR MEMBERS MAGICAL ARMAMENTS TO USE IN THE FIELD.

SO INSTEAD... WE LEAVE IT TO FATE.

YEAH, IT'S KIND OF AN ETHICAL WORK-AROUND...BUT WHADDAYA GONNA DO?

ANYBODY FEELING LUCKY? WANNA TAKE A SPIN?

ME! ME! I'LL GO FIRST!!

KLONK!

WHIRROKK!

KA-CHUNK!

OH! THAT'S THE TRUE HEART CLASP!

IT LOOKS VERY DASHING.

PULLING. IT. OFF.

TRUE HEART
CLASP
+ DESCRIPTION +
→ Magical aid to knowing someone's intentions
→ Stats +2 and advantage on insight checks

ANYBODY WANNA GO NEXT?

I'LL GIVE IT A TRY.

OOF!

WHAD!

I HAVE A COIN.

IT GOES RIGHT INTO THE MACHINE.

RIGHT! HERE YOU GO!

NO, YOU HAVE TO PUT IT IN THE MACHINE YOURSELF.

THERE'S THIS WHOLE THING, LIKE FATE...CHANCE...DIVINE INTERVENTION.

SO WHERE DOES THE COIN GO?

INTO...THE COIN-SHAPED HOLE...

EXCELLENT!

...WHERE?

RIGHT THERE... FRONT OF THE MACHINE.

GOOD NEWS! I'VE SOLVED YOUR PUZZLE!

...YOU'RE... HALFWAY HOME.

NOW JUST... CRANK THE HANDLE TO THE RIGHT.

SORRY, MAN, IT WON'T CRANK!

BECAUSE YOU'RE CRANKING IT TO THE *LEFT!* YOU HAVE TO CRANK IT TO THE *RIGHT!*

I DID AN INSIGHT CHECK. IT LEANED TOWARD THE LEFT.

JUST CRANK IT TO THE RIGHT!!

OOPS.

KUNK

CHA-KUNK!

THAT IS THE RING OF CHILLING FROST.

IT DEFENDS YOU FROM FROST ATTACK, BUT MOST IMPORTANTLY, IF YOU ARE HOLDING ANY BEVERAGE, THE RING MAKES IT VERY FROSTY AND REFRESHING.

SO...A KOOZIE RING.

RING of CHILLING FROST
→ Boost +1 defense from frost attack
→ Other use: good for keggers

...MAGIC DOG...

...MAGIC DOG...

...MAGIC DOG...

CHA-CHUNK!

THUNK!

YOU HOLD IN YOUR HANDS RAILSPLITTER.

DODGE!

IT IS A VERY POWERFUL AX THAT CAN CHOP DOWN ANY TREE WITH A SINGLE SWING.

SINCE IT'S A +1 BATTLE-AX, IT ADDS +1 TO YOUR ATTACK AND DAMAGE.

SWEET!

OOH!

RAILSPLITTER
→ Type: Battle-ax
→ Boost: to attack + damage
→ Other use: limb removal

OKAY. THAT'S IT FOR THE PRETEND MONEY, WHERE DO WE SPEND THE REAL STUFF?

IF YOU LOOK RIGHT...HERE IN YOUR ORIENTATION TIMETABLE, THAT SHOULD BE YOUR NEXT STOP.

COOL.

PLUNK PLUNK

BUT BEFORE WE GO...

...CAN YOU TELL ME...

HOLY SHIT! AN UMBRA STAFF!

SO...

YES?

WHAT AN *INTRIGUING* BUMBERSHOOT YOU HAVE THERE!

DON'T YOU WORRY YOUR FURRY LITTLE SELF ABOUT THAT.

YOU'RE PROVIDING US WITH SHIT. NOT THE OTHER WAY AROUND.

FOR NOW...

SO, YOU MUST BE RECENT HIRES? FIRST DAY ON THE MOON?

ALWAYS GREAT TO SEE NEW BLOOD!

"NEW BLOOD"!!!

HAHA HAHAHA!

SEE, IT'S VERY FUNNY IF YOU KNOW I ACCEPT BLOOD AS CURRENCY.

I JUST KILL ME.

AHEM

ALLOW ME TO SUGGEST...

WEIRD THAT HE KNEW WE HAD EXACTLY 1,800 GOLD.

"ONLY GOOD AT PARTICIPATING OLIVE GARDENS." WHAT A RIP.

...AND I GOT THIS COOL AX! CUTS DOWN ANY TREE WITH ONE SWIPE! DOESN'T IT LOOK AWESOME?!

IT'S A STONE OF FAR*SPEECH*, MAGNUS.

I CAN'T *SEE* YOU.

LISTEN, WE'RE GOING TO HAVE TO INTERRUPT BREAK TIME.

SOME REAL BAD NEWS JUST CAME IN. WE GOTTA SEND YOU ON ANOTHER MISSION.

WHAT, LIKE TOMORROW?

LIKE NOW.

WE HAVEN'T EVEN BEEN TO OUR ROOM!

OR HAD A NIPPY-NAP!

I BOOKED A KELP WRAP AT 4:30!

I'M SORRY, GENTLEMEN.

IT CAN'T BE HELPED.

A FEW DAYS AGO, OUR SEEKERS LOCATED ANOTHER ARTIFACT.

THIS WEAPON IS... EVEN MORE POWERFUL, MORE DANGEROUS THAN THE PHOENIX FIRE GAUNTLET.

WE DISPATCHED ONE OF OUR RECLAIMERS TO RETRIEVE IT—A MAN NAMED LEEMAN KESSLER.

AFTER HIS INITIAL REPORT, LEEMAN VIOLATED PROTOCOL BY NOT CHECKING IN AT THE REQUIRED TIME.

WE FEAR HE WAS UNABLE TO RESIST THE THRALL OF THE ARTIFACT.

YEAH, WELL, NOT EVERYBODY'S TAAKO!

YOU ARE CERTAINLY CORRECT THERE.

WHILE I WAS GETTING YOU LOT SET UP WITH HR, THE BUREAU SENT ONE OF MY FELLOW REGULATORS—CAREY FANGBATTLE—TO RECOVER KESSLER FROM HIS LAST KNOWN LOCATION:

THE CITY OF ROCKPORT.

DID SHE FIND HIM?

YEAH, SHE FOUND HIM.

HE WASN'T *BREATHING*, BUT SHE FOUND HIM.

LET ME GUESS...NO WEAPON.

NO WEAPON.

DID THEY FIND ANYTHING?

A LOT OF BLOOD.

OF COURSE. NOBODY EVER DIES OF OLD AGE AROUND YOU PEOPLE.

ALSO A BAGGAGE CAR CLAIM CHECK...

...AND A TRAIN TICKET FOR THE ROCKPORT LIMITED.

SO...THERE'S NO CHANCE THE ROCKPORT LIMITED IS A CHAIN CLOTHING STORE?

IT'S A TRAIN THAT RUNS FROM ROCKPORT TO EVERSUMMER THROUGH A MOUNTAIN RANGE CALLED "THE TEETH."

WE BELIEVE LEEMAN MANAGED TO SECURE PASSAGE.

THE LUGGAGE CLAIM WOULD INDICATE HE WAS ABLE TO STASH THE ARTIFACT ON THE TRAIN...

BUT HE GOT WHACKED BEFORE THE DEPARTURE.

PUMP THE BRAKES FOR A SECOND THERE, DIRECTOR.

YOU SAID YOU USED SOME HOODOO TO MAKE EVERYONE FORGET THE ARTIFACTS.

IF SO, THEN HOW DID SOMEONE KNOW TO KILL THE VIC AND STEAL THE WEAPON?

WE DON'T KNOW...

HELP US ORGANIZE CAMP GOODENOUGH

WE'RE HOPING IT'S A HORRIBLE COINCIDENCE...

...BECAUSE ANY OTHER ALTERNATIVE IS TOO TERRIFYING TO CONTEMPLATE.

NEVER MIND THAT...

THE TRAIN LEAVES IN TWO HOURS.

ONE OF YOU MUST POSE AS LEEMAN KESS—

GRAB!

FANTASY COSTCO

"ALAS! POOR YOGI! I KNEW HIM, HORSERADISH!"

"A FELLOW WITH INK ON HIS CHEST—"

WE'RE IN KIND OF A RUSH HERE! WE DON'T REALLY HAVE TIME FOR AUDITIONS!

FINE! YOU CAN BE LEEMAN KESSLER!

ACTING! THANK YOU!

hee hee!

YOU NEED TO LOOK LIKE YOU BELONG ON A FANCY TRAIN. GO CHANGE AND THEN GET YOUR ASSES DOWN TO THE HANGAR!

HMMMM... "WARDROBE FITTING."

NOW WE'RE TALKING!

ALL RIGHT, WELL, THE REST OF THIS ORIENTATION AGENDA'S PRETTY MUCH TRASHED.

SO MUCH FOR "MERLE GETS TATTOO REMOVED"!

WHO SCHEDULED THAT?

AND WHY DO THEY HATE KENNY CHESNEY?

"PICK OUT KESSLER PARTY DISGUISES."

CHECK!

"REPORT TO NEW ROOM IN ENTRY-LEVEL DORMS."

CHECK!

"BE UNDERWHELMED"...

CHECK.

THIS CAN'T BE RIGHT.

YOU MUST HAVE BROUGHT US TO THE WRONG PLACE... LIKE...A MOON BASE JAIL CELL.

WHAT? ARE YOU CRAZY? THIS IS *PERFECT!*

THIS IS HOW THEY TREAT HEROES?!

WE BRING THEM A DEADLY FIRE GAUNTLET AND THEY STICK US IN THIS DUMP?

THERE'S NO WAY THEY CAN EXPECT THREE PEOPLE TO LIVE IN THIS ROOM!

THEY DON'T...

...THEY EXPECT *FOUR* PEOPLE TO LIVE IN THIS ROOM.

DON'T TOUCH MY SHIT!! —ROBBIE

UN-BE-LEEV-ABLE!

OH, I DON'T KNOW...

...I KIND OF LIKE HIS STYLE.

HEY, FELLAS!!

THESE DISGUISES ARE *AWESOME!*

OH, YEAH.

I'M GONNA NEED TO LIVE OFF-CAMPUS.

AVI IS WAITING FOR YOU IN THE CANNON BAY.

IF YOU LEAVE NOW YOU SHOULD HAVE JUST ENOUGH TIME TO CLAIM KESSLER'S LUGGAGE BEFORE THE TRAIN LEAVES THE STATION.

YOU CAN USE YOUR BRACERS TO CALL FOR A TRANSPORT SPHERE ONCE YOU HAVE THE ARTIFACT IN HAND.

HOLD UP...

..."CANNON BAY"?

AH.

YES, I SHOULD WARN YOU, THE BUREAU'S MAIN MEANS OF CONVEYANCE IS...

...PRETTY INTENSE.

SHIT...SERIOUSLY? THOSE ARE *TRANSPORTATION* CANNONS?

HUH. I THOUGHT THEY WERE FOR MOON-BASE-TO-MOON-BASE COMBAT OR SOMETHING.

ONE MORE THING...

THE MAGIC USERS WHO CREATED THIS WEAPON...THEY'RE CALLED...RED ROBES, NAMED AFTER THE BRIGHT CRIMSON GARMENTS THEY WEAR.

AS YOU MIGHT GUESS, THEY'RE INCREDIBLY DANGEROUS INDIVIDUALS.

IF YOU COME ACROSS ANY OF THEM IN THIS MISSION, IT'S *IMPERATIVE* THAT YOU—

...

WHAT'S *THIS* ONE DO?!

DOES THIS BAD BOY HAVE NITROUS?!

TOO FAST!! TOO FURIOUS!!

THIS WILL BE A LOT MORE... UNCOMFORTABLE THAN YOUR LAST RIDE. A LOT OF FORCE.

YEAH, YEAH, YEAH! LET'S JUST GET THIS OVER WITH!

I DON'T SEE ANY CUP HOLDERS.

AVI
DESIGNATION
LAUNCH SPECIALIST
+ PROFICIENCIES +
→ PERIGREES
→ APOGEES
→ HERO WORSHIP

BUT LISTEN, IT IS *VITALLY IMPORTANT* THAT ONE OF YOU SIT IN THAT SEAT.

THIS IS A FANTASY AIR BRAKE.

IF YOU PULL IT TOO EARLY, THE MOMENTUM DISRUPTION MAGIC WILL FADE.

AND THAT WOULD BE BAD.

SURE, SURE. GOT IT.

Chapter 2

THANKS TO YOU, O DUNGEON MASTER, WE ARE NOW JACKED!

NO NEED TO THANK ME. YOU EARNED IT.

LIKE UNTO GODS, WE MARCH ON TO ROCKPORT!

TO ROCKPORT!

IT'S, UH, BACK THIS WAY, FELLAS...

AGAIN WITH THE CAVES...

EXCUSE ME, MY GOOD MAN!

MY NAME IS DEFINITELY LEEMAN KESSLER...

AH YES, MR. KESSLER—

~~MERLE~~
LEEMAN
KESSLER
+ PROFICIENCIES +
→ Startling Resemblance to Merle

WE'VE BEEN EXPECTING YOU!

MY NAME IS THOMAS! I AM THE CONCIERGE OF THE ROCKPORT LIMITED!

GEE, THOMAS. JUST THE SOUND OF YOUR VOICE MAKES ME FEEL SO...WELCOME.

THOMAS
RACE HUMAN
CLASS CONCIERGE
+ PROFICIENCIES +
→ Hospitality
→ convenient exposition
→ leaving the light on for ya

AND THESE TWO GENTLEMEN ARE...?

MY RETAINERS... BO AND...DIDDLY.

41

THE FASTEST, MOST POWERFUL TRAIN IN THE REALM!

SHE'LL MAKE THE TWO HUNDRED MILES TO EVERSUMMER IN FOUR HOURS!

THE ULTIMATE IN LUXURY AND COMFORT!

YOU GONNA COMP US SOME SNACKS? MAYBE A TRAY OR THREE OF MOJITOS?

OH, WELL... SURE.

ALL RIGHT!

LET'S GET ON THAT TRAIN!

SLAP!

?

??

SO WE CAN GRAB THE MCGUFFIN, GET THE HELL OUT OF HERE, AND GET BACK TO THE BASE BEFORE KARAOKE NIGHT.

oohhhh!

YES, BY ALL MEANS, MY GOOD MAN! BUT FIRST, I WOULD LIKE TO CHECK ON MY PROPERTY!

YOU'VE GOT A HELL OF A LOT OF ARMED BEEF STATIONED HERE, THOMAS. SOMETHING WE NEED TO KNOW?

OH, NO, SIR, NOTHING TO CONCERN YOURSELVES ABOUT!

NOTHING WRONG HERE! JUST ANOTHER TYPICAL, MURDER-FREE DAY IN ROCKPORT!!

TO LIMIT ACCESS, OUR STATE-OF-THE-ART CARGO CAR IS AT THE VERY REAR OF THE TRAIN.

NO WINDOWS, WHICH KEEPS IT EVEN MORE SECURE FROM MARAUDERS...

...NOT THAT THEY'LL BE ANY PROBLEM...

...THANKS TO THE CRYPTSAFE.

CRYPTSAFE
TOP-OF-THE-LINE SECURITY DEVICE

THE CRYPTSAFE IS INDESTRUCTIBLE AND BUILT INTO THE VERY FLOOR OF THE CAR.

IMPRESSIVE!

LET ME VIEW MY PROPERTY, SIR.

AFRAID THAT'S NOT POSSIBLE, MR. KESSLER. YOUR ITEMS HAVE ALREADY BEEN STOWED IN THE CRYPTSAFE.

IT'S TIME-LOCKED. IT WILL ONLY OPEN AFTER AN EMPLOYEE OF THE RAILROAD—SPECIFICALLY, THE ENGINEER, MR. HUDSON—MAINTAINS SUSTAINED PHYSICAL CONTACT WITH IT...

...FOR AN HOUR.

IT WAS A GOOD THOUGHT.

THOMAS, ABOUT ALL THOSE GUARDS—

OH, MAGNUS. THOMAS IS A VERY BUSY MAN WHOSE CHARM SPELL IS GOING TO WEAR OFF ANY SECOND NOW.

IN THE INTEREST OF TYING UP LOOSE ENDS, WE COULD TELL HIM TO STEP IN FRONT OF THE TRAIN...?

NO.

WE'VE GOT MORE IMPORTANT SHIT TO WORRY ABOUT!

LIKE THE FACT THAT THE ARTIFACT WE'RE SUPPOSED TO GET IS HEADED TO EVERSUMMER WITH OR WITHOUT US!!

SOUNDS LIKE THE THREE OF US WILL HAVE TO RIDE ALONG IF WE'RE GOING TO SECURE THE PAYLOAD.

AND I DOUBT THERE'S ANY STONE RECEPTION IN THOSE MOUNTAINS...SO NO HELP FROM THE BUREAU PEOPLE, EITHER. WE'RE ON OUR OWN.

IN THAT CASE, YOU TWO ARE GOING TO HAVE TO DO A BETTER JOB OF STAYING IN CHARACTER!

HAVE YOU GIVEN THE SLIGHTEST THOUGHT TO YOUR MOTIVATION?

ALL ABOOOOAARD!!! TIME TO GET YOUR ASSES ON THE TRAIN THAT I SPENT *HOURS COMING UP WITH!*

OR YOUR INNER MONOLOGUE?!

IS THAT SHAG CARPET?

THIS IS A FULL-OPTION TRAIN, MY DUDES, FULLY LUXURIED OUT.

THIS IS THE LEXUS OF FANTASY TRAINS. GILDED FEATURES. POSH INTERIOR.

YES, IT IS. GOOD EYE, SIR.

I AM HUDSON, YOUR ENGINEER. WELCOME ABOARD. WE'RE HAPPY TO HAVE YOU.

HUDSON,
Race   ELF
Class   ENGINEER
(NOT THE BRIDGE-BUILDING,
TUNNEL-DIGGING KIND...THE
"MAKING THE TRAIN GO" KIND)
+ PROFICIENCIES +
→ Toeing the corporate line
→ Railway navigation
→ Doing the Loco-motion

WE KNOW YOU HAVE A LOT OF CHOICES FOR SUBTERRANEAN INTER-CITY TRAVEL, AND WE APPRECIATE THAT YOU CHOSE US!

WELL, THANK YOU FOR HAVING US ON YOUR EXQUISITE CHOO-CHOO.

YOU'RE IN LUCK. WE'RE RIDING LIGHT, SO YOU'LL HAVE YOUR PICK OF SEATING IN THE PASSENGER CAR.

AND HERE WE ARE AT THE ENGINE CAR. THIS IS WHERE I WILL BE FOR THE DURATION OF THE TRIP.

AS A SECURITY MEASURE, I WILL NOT BE COMING OUT AGAIN UNTIL WE ARRIVE AT EVERSUMMER.

THIS IS ALSO WHERE I MUST ASK YOU FOR—

OUR TICKETS? OF COURSE!

NO, SIR.

YOUR WEAPONS, PLEASE.

UHHH...NO.

NO, THANK YOU. I DON'T BELIEVE I WANT TO DO THAT.

MOUNTAIN TRAIN SECURITY AGENCY PROTOCOLS DEMAND THAT ALL WEAPONS BE LOCKED UP WITH ME IN THE ENGINE CAR.

GOODBYE, SMOOSHER.

GOODBYE, LIL CHOPPY.

IS IT OKAY IF I KEEP MY UMBRELLA IN CASE OF A STORM?

WELL, WE'LL BE INSIDE A TRAIN INSIDE A GIANT MOUNTAIN RANGE, SO NOT MUCH CHANCE OF RAIN, BUT...SURE!

VISIT SCENIC GOLDCLIFF

PAID FOR BY THE GOLDCLIFF TRUST

ALL RIGHT, BUT I HAVE TO HANG ON TO MY GAUNTLET. I HAVE...STINKY HAND SYNDROME.

HE'S NOT KIDDING. THE STENCH WILL HAUNT YOUR DREAMS.

FINE.

BUT YOU HAVE TO DO ONE THING FOR ME!

WHAT'S THAT?

LET ME SIT ON YOUR LAP AND STEER?

WHOOMSHLAM!

HUDSON THE ENGINEER, LADIES AND GENTLEMEN!!

WE HOPE YOU ENJOYED HIM! WE'LL SEE HIM AGAIN AT THE END OF THE LINE!

HE WASN'T KIDDING ABOUT IT NOT BEING VERY FULL.

AND TWO OF THEM ARE DWARVES!

LOOK CLOSER...

...I THINK THE LITTLEST ONE IS A KID.

YOU DON'T THINK THAT'S WEIRD? SOME LITTLE KID TRAVELING BY HIMSELF ON A TRAIN?

HE'S PERFECTLY FINE, SIR...

...THE ROCKPORT LIMITED IS PERFECTLY SAFE.

MY NAME IS JENKINS. YOUR WIZARD ATTENDANT FOR THIS TRIP.

JENKINS
RACE ELF
CLASS
EITHER a
WIZARD WHO'S
an attendant
OR an attendant
TO WIZARDS
+ PROFICIENCIES +
+ GASTRONOMY
+ PERSONAL SERVICE
+ HORTICULTURE

I LIKE YOUR TIE, JENKINS. TELL ME ABOUT IT.

YOU HAVE AN EYE FOR THE FINER THINGS, SIR.

THIS IS MY... FLAIR. WE ALL GET TO WEAR ONE PIECE OF FLAIR ON TUESDAYS.

GOOD GOD! MORE BUNK BEDS!

IT'S AS IF EVERY DECORATOR IN THIS REALITY SPENT WAY TOO MUCH TIME AT SUMMER CAMP!

SO ARE YOU AN ATTENDANT WHO'S A WIZARD, OR AN ATTENDANT *TO* A WIZARD—

I AM A WIZARD WHO MUST ATTEND TO THE NEEDS OF THE PASSENGERS ON THE TRAIN.

AND I HAVE A FEW LUXURY SERVICES I CAN PROVIDE.

FOR INSTANCE, I CAN TAKE YOU INTO OUR PLEASURE CHAMBER.

SORRY TO DISAPPOINT, BUT IT'S NOT A SEX THING.

MY SOFT, SENSUOUS VOICE JUST MAKES EVERYTHING SOUND SALACIOUS. IT'S A CURSE.

THE PLEASURE CHAMBER IS A RECREATIONAL TELEPORTATION EXPERIENCE THAT ALLOWS PASSENGERS TO BRIEFLY VISIT ANY ENCLOSED SPACE OF THEIR CHOOSING ANYWHERE IN THE WORLD.

THE SPELL IS POWERFUL BUT LIMITED. YOU CAN'T BRING ANYTHING BACK THROUGH THE PORTAL...OR LEAVE ANYTHING THERE.

JUST IN CASE YOU WERE THINKING OF DOING ANY, YOU KNOW, SMUGGLING.

LEEMAN KESSLER IS NO SMUGGLER!!

LIKE YOU'D KNOW.

I SAW A DWARVEN WOMAN IN THE PASSENGER CAR AND I SWEAR I RECOGNIZED HER.

I'M NOT SUPPOSED TO SHARE PRIVILEGED INFORMATION REGARDING THE IDENTITY OF—

COME ON, JENKINS, OLD BUDDY...

I AM NOT YOUR... "BUDDY"!

OH, COME ON, JENKIE!

ALL RIGHT!

BUT YOU DIDN'T HEAR THIS FROM ME.

THAT'S...

...JESS THE BEHEADER.

JESS

Race DWARF
Class PROFESSIONAL WRESTLER

+ Proficiencies +
→ Pride in Profession
→ avoiding the Public
→ Well, there's the whole "beheading thing"

HOLY SHIT!! IT IS!!

SHE LOOKS TOTALLY DIFFERENT WITHOUT HER GRAPPLING GARB!!

"GRAPPLING GARB"? DON'T TELL ME YOU'RE A WRESTLING FAN!!

DON'T YOU KNOW THAT'S JUST A BUNCH OF MADE-UP FANTASY BULLSHIT?

YES, I'M SURE YOU WOULD. BUT THERE'S NO CHANCE OF THAT DURING THIS TRIP.

IT'S LOCKED UP WITH HUDSON. I HAD TO LUG THE DAMNED THING UP THERE MYSELF.

KIND OF A SHITTY WIZARD.

I'M SORRY...SIR?

JUST CAST A SPELL OF LEVITATION! THAT'S SECOND LEVEL STUFF, MY MAN!

OH, I'M SORRY.

WHAT AM I GOING TO DO? BURN ONE OF MY DAILY SLOTS ON LEVITATING AN AX?

I DIDN'T REALIZE THAT LIFE ON THE RAILS WAS SO *DEMANDING* YOU NEED PYROTECHNICS AT YOUR FINGERTIPS TWENTY-FOUR-SEV!

YOU SHOULD DO WHAT I DO: HAVE UNLIMITED SPELL SLOTS AND USE EVERY SPELL IN THE BOOK!

THAT'S CALLED "CHEATING," ACTUALLY.

YEAH...WELL...

WE WOULDN'T WANT TO DO THAT... WOULD WE?

MAYBE YOU JUST NEED TO LIVE LIFE A LITTLE! GET OUT IN THE WORLD AND LEVEL UP! THAT'S ALL I'M SAYING.

I HAVE NO INTEREST IN YOUR LIFE HACKS.

BACK THERE IS THE KITCHEN.

I AM ALSO THE CHEF ON THIS TRIP. NOW THAT I KNOW YOU, I'LL BE SURE TO BAKE A LOT OF LOVE INTO WHATEVER YOU ORDER.

YOU SAVING YOUR SPELLS FOR THAT?

OF COURSE, BEYOND THE KITCHEN IS THE CARGO CAR. I'M SURE YOU'VE BEEN BRIEFED ON ALL THE SECURITY PROTOCOLS.

NO DOUBT MOST OF IT SAILED OVER YOUR HEADS—

JENKINS, COULD YOU PLEASE OPEN THE WINDOW?

CERTAINLY, SIR.

BUT BY ALL MEANS, DON'T BURN A SPELL SLOT ON IT.

HA!

NOW SEE HERE!

I LIVE TO SERVE THE PEOPLE ON THIS TRAIN! AND YOU CRETINS—!!

EASY, JENKINS! WE'RE JUST JOSHIN'!

PLEASE, GENTLEMEN, WE REALLY MUST MOVE AHEAD WITH THE TOUR.

IT'S NEARLY NOON...

...AND THAT'S "JENKINS' TIME."

AS IN—?

AS IN "JENKINS' TIME...

"...YOUR BRUNCH."

"...TO START FIXING...

SLAM!!

Chapter 3

EXCUSE ME, FANCY LAD...

CALEB CLEVEL AND THE TOMB OF HO

HOW WOULD YOU LIKE TO BE A "PAN-CY" LAD?

PAN FOLD

BE A FAN OF PAN

I'D LIKE TO TELL YOU ABOUT MY GOOD FRIEND PAN.

ESPECIALLY ONES WHO WORSHIP OLYMPIAN GODS.

THANK YOU FOR THE EVANGELISM, SIR, BUT MY GRANDPA ALWAYS TOLD ME I SHOULDN'T TALK TO STRANGERS...

WELL, I NOTICED YOU'RE READING. PERHAPS YOU'D LIKE TO READ THIS CHICK TRACT.

YOU CAN CALL ME BROTHER LEEMAN.

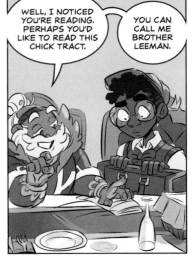

THIS KID IS DEFINITELY THE BAD GUY.

MY NAME'S ANGUS. ANGUS MCDONALD.

I'M GOING TO VISIT MY GRANDPA IN EVERSUMMER.

ANGUS MCDONALD
RACE HUMAN
CLASS
unaccompanied minor
+ PROFICIENCIES +
→ Being adorable
→ Reading at a high school level
→ Snack consumption

I CAN'T WAIT TO READ YOUR VERY SMALL PAMPHLET DRAWN IN A SIMPLE STYLE REMINISCENT OF UNDERGROUND COMICS! I LOVE TO READ!

SEE? WHAT LITTLE KID LIKES TO READ?!

HE IS SO-O-O-O THE BAD GUY.

IF YOU SIRS WILL EXCUSE ME...

I CAME HERE TO READ BOOKS AND CHEW BUBBLE GUM, AND I'M ALL OUT OF GUM.

THANK YOU FOR THE GOOD CHAT.

WOW...

...THIS THING'S AMAZING!

THIS *TRAIN* IS AMAZING!!

DON'T YOU GUYS LOVE BEING ON THIS TRAIN? THIS TRAIN'S THE BEST!

EH, I'VE SEEN BETTER.

MY NAME'S GRAHAM. AND YOU ARE...?

GRAHAM
RACE HUMAN
CLASS WIZARD
+ PROFICIENCIES +
+ Train obssession
+ Dodgy fashion choices
+ Panic

I'M LEEMAN KESSLER. AND THESE ARE MY ATTENDANTS: FLHOMAS—

DIDDLY.

—OF COURSE, DIDDLY. AND THIS IS—

JUSTIN!

~~FLHOMAS~~ ~~RHOMAS~~ ~~FLHOMAS~~ DIDDLY

~~TAAKO~~ ~~LEMAN KESSLER~~ ~~SEXY~~ I QUIT!! —PERSON WRITING THESE CHARACTER SHEETS!!

I CAN'T HELP BUT NOTICE YOUR GARB. YOUR HAT AND ALL.

ARE YOU PERCHANCE A WIZARD, TOO?

YEAH. NO DOUBT YOU RECOGNIZE ME.

I'M ACTUALLY TAAKO. YOU KNOW, FROM TV.

YES IT IS, MY DUDE.

HOLY SHIT! IT IS YOU!

WHEN I TRAVEL I USE MY REAL NAME...JUSTIN KESSLER.

YOUR SHOW IS LIKE, MY SECOND FAVORITE THING IN THE WORLD.

IT'S ALWAYS GOOD TO MEET A FAN—

WAIT! *SECOND?!* WHAT'S *FIRST?*

TRAINS!

I WOULD LOVE TO WORK ON A TRAIN. IT'S BEEN MY DREAM TO LIVE A LIFE ON THE RAILS!

AS A MATTER OF FACT, I APPLIED FOR A JOB WITH THE ROCKPORT LIMITED BUT DIDN'T GET ACCEPTED.

MOTIVE! HE HAD MOTIVE!

MOTIVE FOR *WHAT?*

MURDER! *MURDER MOST FOUL.*

OH, SLOW YOUR ROLL, COLUMBO.

I JUST CAME ON THIS TRIP TO SHADOW JENKINS AND SEE WHAT I COULD LEARN. PICK UP FEW POINTERS.

YOU MEAN.. YOU'RE A WORSE WIZARD...THAN *JENKINS?*

I'M STANDING *RIGHT HERE!*

YOU PURPOSELY SAID THAT LOUD ENOUGH FOR ME TO HEAR! WHY WOULD YOU DO THAT?!

I WAS BEING THOUGHTFUL!

I DIDN'T WANT YOU TO WASTE A *PRECIOUS SPELL SLOT* TRYING TO READ MY MIND!

AWK-WARD...

CRUNCH CRUMPLE

SLURP

WE ARE REEEEALLY MAKING FRIENDS ON THIS TRAIN.

I HAD A TRICKED-OUT WAGON, PULLED BY A COUPLE OF BEAUTIFUL HORSES: ALTON AND NIGELLA.

I JUST HAD TO HIT A COUPLE OF SWITCHES AND VOILÀ! MY WHOLE SETUP, RIGHT THERE ON THE ROAD!

AHHHH, IT WAS A THING OF BEAUTY, MERLE!

THE WHOLE RIG WAS PRETTY PRICEY, BUT IT WAS WORTH EVERY CENT.

OH! IT WAS A MONEY-MAKING THING!

I THOUGHT IT WAS SOME KIND OF ART FORM!

IT WAS, THE WAY *I* DID IT!

UH, HELLO?

ISN'T IT TIME WE GOT BACK TO SOLVING *THE CASE?!*

GIVE IT A REST!!

PLEASURE CHAMBER
+ POWER +
+ TRANSPORT
TO OTHER LOCATIONS
+ IT TOTALLY CaN Be a
SEX THING

FOR SUCH A SOPHISTICATED TELEPORTATION MAGIC, YOU'D HAVE TO USE SOMETHING TO FOCUS IT...

TAP TAP

TELEPORT ROD?

YES INDEED. IT WORKS IN CONCERT WITH THE CHAMBER.

THAT'S AN ASTUTE OBSERVATION FOR HIRED MUSCLE.

JENKINS, OLD PAL—

TELEPORT ROD

+POWER+
activates
teleportation
magic

CALEB CLEVELAN AND THE TOMB OF HORR

DON'T JUDGE A BOOK BY ITS BREATHTAKINGLY ATTRACTIVE COVER.

WHAT WILL IT BE, GENTLEMEN?

A DAY SPA AT SWORD BEACH? THE MINSKER POOL HALL IN GOLDCLIFF?

I KNOW!

I WANT YOU TO SEND ME...

TO OUR SLEEPER CAR!

HERE   SNRK

YOU WANT ME TO USE... MY INCREDIBLE TELEPORTATION MAGIC...

TO GO INTO THE ROOM THAT IS ADJACENT TO THE ROOM WE'RE CURRENTLY IN?

HELLO, SIRS.

HOW WAS YOUR TRIP?

VERY PLEASURABLE! BUT WE SURE MISSED **YOU.**

YOU DID? THAT'S NICE, SIRS!

AND SINCE WE'RE ALL GETTING SO CLOSE...

...MAYBE YOU WOULD BE WILLING TO TELL ME YOUR **REAL** NAMES?

SAY WHA-?

'SCUSE?

WHAT DO YOU MEAN, PUMPKIN?

YOUR **REAL** NAMES. WHAT YOU CALL YOURSELF WHEN YOU'RE **NOT** PRETENDING TO BE LEEMAN KESSLER.

WHO WAS MURDERED RECENTLY, DID YOU KNOW THAT?

WE KNOW THAT. HOW DO **YOU** KNOW THAT?

BECAUSE I'M...

-the WORLD'S GREATEST DETECTIVE!!!

ANGUS McDONALD
Race HUMAN
CLass WORLD'S GREATEST detective (SELF-PROCLaimed)
+ PROFICIENCIES +
→ Keen Observation
→ Analytical mind
→ Keeping secrets

...TO PARSE THE RELEVANT MESSAGE.

THOMAS 13:05:02

LEEMAN KESSLER AND CO. NOT WHO THEY SAY THEY ARE -STOP- CHARM MAGIC SPELL PERFORMED ON ME AT THE STATION -STOP- HAND OVER TO AUTHORITIES IMMEDIATELY UPON ARRIVAL IN EVERSUMMER -STOP-

CRITERIA:
☑ HAS PASS NAMES
☑ ROCKPORT GMC

(MESSAGES FOUND: 1)

HANG ON, IS THIS SUPPOSED TO BE USEFUL? I CAN'T MAKE IT OUT AT *ALL!*

WELL, OF COURSE— THE BOOK PICKS UP AN UNFILTERED MAGICAL STREAM!

I SIMPLY FILTERED OUT ANYTHING WITH AN ORIGIN BEYOND ROCKPORT'S GEOMAGICAL COORDINATES, CLUSTERED RECORDS SENT WITHIN THE PERIOD JUST BEFORE EMBARKATION, TWEAKED A BASIC NLP TOOLKIT TO FLAG ANY UNEXPECTED REFERENCES TO PASSENGERS, AND APPLIED THAT TO THE INCOMING DATA...

WELL, IF IT WERE EASY, YOU WOULDN'T HAVE TO BE THE WORLD'S GREATEST DETECTIVE TO USE IT!!

I *KNEW* WE SHOULD HAVE MADE THAT THOMAS GUY WALK IN FRONT OF A TRAIN!

THIS KID SEEMS TO HAVE HIS SHIT TOGETHER. HE COULD BE A REAL ASSET TO ME AS I SOLVE THIS MYSTERY.

YOU SOLVE—

ALL RIGHT, KID...

...LET'S GO HAVE A PRIVATE CONVO.

Chapter 4

MY NAME'S TAAKO. YOU PROBABLY RECOGNIZE ME—

FROM TV, YES, I AM FAMILIAR, SIR.

SO.

WHAT'S THE SKINNY, KID? YOU CAN LEVEL WITH ME.

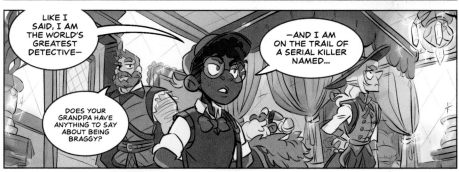

LIKE I SAID, I AM THE WORLD'S GREATEST DETECTIVE—

—AND I AM ON THE TRAIL OF A SERIAL KILLER NAMED...

DOES YOUR GRANDPA HAVE ANYTHING TO SAY ABOUT BEING BRAGGY?

—the— ROCKPORT SLAYER.

WAIT A SEC! SERIAL KILLER? YOU'RE LIKE *EIGHT!* SHOULDN'T YOU BE FIGURING OUT WHO STOLE THE MONEY FROM LITTLE SUZIE'S LEMONADE STAND?

I'M *TEN.*

THE ROCKPORT CITY COUNCIL WANTS ME TO TRACK DOWN THE PERSON WHO HAS BEEN KILLING LOCAL WEALTHY INDIVIDUALS FOR THE PAST FEW MONTHS.

THE SLAYER MURDERS THEM AND STEALS THEIR RICHES...AND NEVER LEAVES A TRACE.

GOOD LUCK! -R.C.C.

BUT *I* AM GOING TO *STOP* THIS LUNATIC!

YES...*WE* WILL STOP THAT LUNATIC.

WE'LL HAVE TO LOOK AT OUR SUSPECT LIST.

I GUESS A TRIO OF DESPERATE HARD-ASSES LIKE US ARE RIGHT AT THE TOP OF THAT LIST, HUH, KID?

OH, NO, SIR.

I AM A HUNDRED PERCENT SURE THAT THE THREE OF YOU DON'T POSSESS THE COMPETENCY REQUIRED TO PERFORM MULTIPLE MURDERS WITHOUT GETTING CAUGHT.

PRETTY SOLID OBSERVATION.

HE *IS* A GOOD DETECTIVE!

HOWEVER, THE FACT THAT YOU SHOWED UP POSING AS LEEMAN KESSLER INDICATES YOU ARE ALSO LOOKING FOR HIS KILLER...

...OR HIS TREASURE!

YOU TOLD HIM THERE'S A TREASURE?!

I DIDN'T SAY NUTHIN' ABOUT NO TREASURE!

WHY DO YOU THINK THERE'S A TREASURE?

THAT'S THE ROCKPORT SLAYER'S M.O.

HE KILLS, THEN STEALS HIS VICTIM'S MOST VALUABLE POSSESSION...

...AND THAT'S WHY YOU'RE ON THE TRAIN.

I THINK WE'RE WORKING TOWARD A SIMILAR GOAL.

THE THREE OF US WORK FOR AN ORGANIZATION—

WHAT ORGANIZATION? FANTASY C.S.I.? FANTASY S.H.I.E.L.D.? FANTASY MALL COPS?

THE BUREAU OF BALANCE.

...I... COULDN'T QUITE CATCH THAT, SIR...?

NOT THIS SHIT AGAIN...

I WOULD BE WILLING TO BET THAT WE ALSO CAN'T TELL YOU THAT WE'RE TRYING TO RECOVER "A DANGEROUS MAGICAL ARTIFACT"!

"DANGEROUS MAGICAL ARTIFACT," GOT YOU LOUD AND CLEAR!

HM...SO THERE'S THIS *MOON BASE* AND DOGS AREN'T ALLOWED THERE...?

FWUMP.

DO THOSE COMMUNICATION BRACERS PREVENT ME FROM UNDERSTANDING WHAT YOU ARE TRYING TO SAY?

SURE, LET'S GO WITH THAT.

ANGUS, HERE'S WHAT WE *CAN* TELL YOU:

THIS ITEM, IF IT FALLS INTO THE WRONG HANDS, IS REMARKABLY DANGEROUS. IT'S *INCREDIBLY* BAD.

THE BODY COUNT FOR THIS SLAYER PERSON WOULD INCREASE FROM DOZENS TO *THOUSANDS* IN SHORT ORDER.

WE NEED TO WORK TOGETHER AND FIGURE THIS OUT *NOW!*

I AGREE. THAT'S WHY I'M ENLISTING YOU TO HELP ME APPREHEND THE ROCKPORT SLAYER...

WHO MUST BE SOMEWHERE ON THIS TRAIN!

IF MY SUSPICIONS ARE TO BE BELIEVED, THE ITEM YOU SEEK IS INSIDE THE CARGO CAR CRYPTSAFE.

BRUSH BRUSH

NOW YOU'RE JUST SHOWBOATING, KID. THAT'S WHERE THEY LOCK STUFF UP ON THIS TRAIN.

YOU DIDN'T REALLY, LIKE, DEDUCE THE SHIT OUT OF THAT ONE.

DULY NOTED, SIRS.

BUT I SUSPECT IT WILL REQUIRE EVERY ONE OF MY LITTLE GRAY CELLS...

...TO IDENTIFY THE ROCKPORT SLAYER.

87

95

WOW!! JESS CRITS FOR 29 POINTS OF DAMAGE!

CRAB CRIT!

THAT WAS SWEET AS HELL!!

YOU CUT IT RIGHT DOWN TO THE WIRE!!

HOW'D YOU KNOW *EXACTLY* THE COOLEST MOMENT TO JUMP IN?

EH, IT LOOKED LIKE YOU GUYS HAD IT HANDLED.

AND I HAD A REALLY BAD INITIATIVE ROLL.

ME TOO!

ME THREE!

NOOOO!! I JUST THOUGHT UP SOME GREAT CRAB PUNS!

OH, ALL RIGHT YOU THREE SCAMPS... LET IT OUT.

ffwwwwssssh!

THAT SURE WAS A KRUSTY KRAB!

WE DID A CLAW-SOME JOB!

JESS WAS KINDA SHELLFISH, KILLING IT LIKE THAT!

ANNND WE'RE DONE.

Chapter 5

MS. BEHEADER, MAY I JUST SAY: I LOVE YOUR WORK!

I HAD BOTH OF YOUR ACTION FIGURES: THE CHAMPIONSHIP BELT VERSION AND THE HARD-TO-FIND BLOOD-SPLATTERED VERSION!

ALWAYS NICE TO MEET A FAN.

I HAVE TO SAY, THAT "GLOWING SPIRITUAL AX" THING WAS PRETTY DAMN SWEET!

KID HAS A CROSSBOW. SHE'S GOT AN AX...PRETTY FLEXIBLE NO-WEAPONS POLICY THIS TRAIN HAS!

OH, IT'S NOT SPIRITUAL, IT'S JUST SOULBOUND TO ME. I CAN SUMMON IT WHENEVER I NEED IT.

CAN I TRY IT?

...IT'S NOT SOULBOUND TO YOU.

WE CAN DO THE BLOOD BROTHER THING! CUT OUR PALMS, SHAKE HANDS...THEN I'LL BE SOULBOUNDED, TOO, RIGHT?

...NO.

BESIDES, THE AX IS KINDA MY "JAM."

EVERYBODY IN THE MIDWORLD WRESTLING FEDERATION HAS A GIMMICK.

MINE HAPPENS TO BE A MAGNIFICENT SOULBOUND AX THAT SPRINGS TO MY SIDE WHEN THERE'S GREAT DANGER.

YEAAAHHH.

CAN'T HELP BUT NOTICE...

...IT'S STILL HERE.

ARE YOU GUYS *SURE* WE HAVE TO STOP USING OUR COVER IDENTITIES?

YES YESYESYES YESYES.

A THOUSAND TIMES YES.

WELL, POOP.

LET'S BE HONEST, MERLE...

...WE NEVER REALLY STARTED.

GRAHAM?

GRAAAAA-HAAAAM?

GRAAAHAM, IT'S TIME TO GET UP.

BAP.

WHAT THE HELL, MAN!! I WAS *AWAKE!!!* WHY DID YOU PUNCH ME?

THAT WASN'T A PUNCH...THAT WAS LIKE...A GENTLE TAP.

BULL! YOU HIT ME WITH LIKE 20% OF YOUR STRENGTH!

NO, GRAHAM, NO. IF IT HAD BEEN 20% YOU'D BE *DEAD.*

IT WAS 3%, TOPS! WITH MY LEFT HAND!

IT STILL REALLY HURT!

LISTENNN, I'M SORRY ABOUT MY PARTNER.

SHOVE

HE CAN COME ON A LITTLE STRONG.

SLIIIDEEEE!

MAGNUS HERE IS A LOOSE CANNON.

GIVE ME SOMETHING TO WORK WITH. HELP *ME* HELP *YOU!*

WHAT'S HE DOING?

GOOD ADVENTURER/BAD ADVENTURER.

WHAT ABOUT *ME?*

HALF A BAD ADVENTURER.

HALF A BAD ADVENTURER WITH *SPELLS!*

I CAST "ZONE OF—"!

AGAIN?! ARE YOU SHITTING ME?!

YOU KNOW YOU CAN BUFF, RIGHT? FOR CRYIN' OUT LOUD, YOU CAN SHOOT FIERY BEAMS OF PURIFYING SANCTIFIED LIGHT! YOU'RE JUST GONNA BE "THE ZONE OF TRUTH" GUY?

IT'S THE ONLY SPELL I SEEM TO BE HALFWAY DECENT AT...

BUT IF YOU INSIST...

...I WITHDRAW MY SUGGESTION.

WE FOUND YOU IN THE CONNECTING CAR WITH JENKINS' CORPSE. DID YOU SEE WHAT HAPPENED?

I WENT TO FIND JENKINS TO ASK HIM IF I COULD TAKE ANOTHER ROUND IN THE PLEASURE CHAMBER.

I OPENED THE DOOR AND SAW A CORPSE ON... ON THE GROUND WITHOUT A...

...A...

ahhhhh

YOU DON'T GET OUT OF THIS BY FAINTING, JUICY!

BWAP.

3.5%.

WHEN YOU SAW THE BODY...DID IT HAVE HANDS?

NO! IT WAS AWFUL!

AND I'D SEEN JENKINS ONLY A FEW MINUTES EARLIER, PROVIDING DRINK SERVICE...

LISTEN TO ME CAREFULLY, BECAUSE THIS NEXT PART IS EXTREMELY IMPORTANT.

DID YOU NOTICE JENKINS SETTING ASIDE ANY DRINKS FOR SOMEONE?

OR DID ANYONE TAKE AN EXTRA DRINK FOR LATER?

IS THERE SOMEWHERE ON THIS TRAIN I CAN FIND SOME DRINKS!!!

THE DRINK CART?!!!

THE DRINK CART IS GONE!

GONE!!

IT'S HITTING US ALL PRETTY HARD, BUD.

WE'LL HAVE TO HELP EACH OTHER THROUGH THIS.

HE'S TELLING THE TRUTH.

I WAS HERE THE WHOLE TIME.

GRAHAM WALKED BACK THERE AND WENT THROUGH THE DOOR.

WHEN THE DOOR SHUT I HEARD A SHRIEK...LIKE SOME SMALL CHILD. THOUGHT HE WAS JUST HAVING A CONNIPTION.

YOU, UHH.

DIDN'T HAPPEN TO... MURDER JENKINS, DID YOU, JESS?

EX*CUSE* ME?

I ONLY ASK BECAUSE OF THE WHOLE "BEHEADER" THING...

...YOU KNOW: JESS THE *BEHEADER*...? JUST TRYING TO BE THOROUGH.

IT'S A STAGE NAME! FOR THE JOB! WHAT DO *YOU* DO FOR A LIVING?

DO YOU "WIZARD" IN YOUR FREE TIME? I ONLY BEHEAD PEOPLE WHEN I *NEED* TO!

I'M A CHEF...UH, WIZARD. SORT OF A CHEF-WIZARD HYBRID.

OR WHEN I'M GETTING PAID FOR IT...

...YOU KNOW...FOR ENTERTAINMENT.

THIS IS GOOD! THIS IS GOOD!

SHOVE!

THE THREE OF US WERE WITH ANGUS, JESS AND GRAHAM WERE TOGETHER IN THE PASSENGER CAR...

AND JENKINS WAS SERVING THEM DRINKS—

YEAH, RIGHT AFTER HE TOOK THE DRINK CART UP TO THE ENGINEER CAR.

HELLOOOO THERE, MISTER—?

HUDSON.

HUDSON. MISTER HUDSON? GOT A SEC?

-SQUAWK- EVERYTHING GOING OKAY BACK THERE?

UMM—

WE SHOULD BE THERE IN ABOUT AN HOUR. PRETTY SMOOTH TRIP SO FAR.

YEAH, ABOUT THAT...

...JENKINS IS DEAD.

JENK—... JENKINS?

THE GUY WITH THE BOW TIE...?

JENKINS WAS A DEDICATED EMPLOYEE OF—

YES. NOW HE'S JUST A *DEAD* EMPLOYEE, AND YOU NEED TO GET OUT HERE.

WELL... THAT'S NOT GOING TO HAPPEN.

WE NEED YOU TO GET OUR ITEMS OUT OF THE MAGIC VAULT THING!

I'D HAVE TO KEEP MY HANDS ON THE CRYPTSAFE FOR AN HOUR TO OPEN IT!

IN AN HOUR WE'LL BE IN EVERSUMMER!

AT LEAST HAND OUT OUR WEAPONS!

NOT A CHANCE!

IF JENKINS IS DEAD, HOW DO I EVEN KNOW YOU THREE DIDN'T KILL HIM?

COME ON OUT HERE AND WE'LL PINKY-SWEAR WE DIDN'T!

OH, PINKY-SWEAR. WHY DIDN'T YOU JUST SAY THAT TO START WITH?

NO!! I'M NOT OPENING THIS DOOR. I CAN'T HELP YOU.

CAN'T, OR WON'T?

INSTEAD OF BEING A CONDUCTOR, YOU SHOULD BE A CAN-DUCTOR.

I'M NOT A CONDUCTOR, I'M AN ENGINEER—

WOULDN'T IT BE NICER TO BE A FRIEND-GINEER?

I'LL TELL YOU WHAT I WANT TO BE—

A GUY WITH HIS HEAD.

BUH-BYE!

GREAT!

TELL US!

ISN'T IT MORE FUN IF YOU FIGURE IT OUT FOR YOURSELVES?

NO, AS A MATTER OF FACT, IT ISN'T!

SO, IS IT—

I DON'T ACTUALLY KNOW!! I WAS TRYING TO IMPRESS YOU!!

I THOUGHT YOU WERE THE WORLD'S GREATEST DETECTIVE!

YEAH, BUT I'M NOT *PSYCHIC!*

EXCUSES, EXCUSES.

ALL-RIGHTY, THEN. YOUR TURN, JESS. SHOW US WHAT'S IN YOUR POCKETS.

UHHHHH...

NO.

SHE'S THREATENING ME! YOU ALL SAW IT!!

WAIT A MINUTE, WAIT A MINUTE, WAIT A MINUTE!

JESS DOESN'T HAVE ANY BLOOD ON HER....!

A FEW FLECKS OF CRAB MEAT, MAYBE, BUT HER ARMOR LOOKS IMPECCABLE—

LOVE THE FIT, BY THE WAY.

YOU'VE *GOT* TO INTRODUCE ME TO YOUR BLACKSMITH.

PEW ✦ ✦ PEW!

AND BECAUSE OF THAT WONDERFUL FIT, I'M PRETTY SURE SHE DOESN'T HAVE ANY POCKETS TO TURN OUT.

OH, SHIT, RIGHT! THAT, TOO!

DAMN! I REALLY THOUGHT THAT WAS GOING TO WORK. NOW WHAT?

WAIT!

I ACTUALLY HAVE A SPELL THAT WILL HELP!

I CAST DISCERNMENT OF MAGICKS!

DISCERNMENT of MAGICKS

hoity-toity way of saying "locate things with magic all over them"

HEY, ARE THOSE MAGICAL LOAFERS?

YEAH...BUT DON'T BRING IT UP.

WELL, NO SIGN OF THE ROD...THAT MEANS NO KILLER.

ONLY ONE PLACE LEFT TO CHECK—

THE CARGO CAR!

skuddle SNUGGLE!

skuddle-BUZZZZ!

SKUDDY SKUDDY SKUDDLE!

WHY DOES IT HAVE TO FEEL SO STICKY?

HOW'S THE ODD COUPLE BACK THERE?

GRAHAM HASN'T SHUT UP SINCE WE LEFT.

RIGHT NOW HE'S ASKING JESS TO BE CAREFUL WITH THE AX BECAUSE HE'S A BLEEDER.

HEE HEE!

WELL, WASN'T THAT ANTICLIMACTIC.

I THINK I SUFFERED A PULLED GROIN KICKING THAT DOOR. I FEEL A LITTLE NAUSEOUS.

WEIRD. ALL OF A SUDDEN, I DON'T HEAR GRAHAM AND JESS ANYMORE.

NOTHING! THERE'S NOTHING ELSE IN HERE!

I WONDER IF DOVES ARE GOOD EATIN'?

THE DRUMSTICKS WOULD BE AWFULLY SMALL...

WAIT JUST A DAMN SECOND!

TO OPEN THE CRYPTSAFE, A ROCKPORT EMPLOYEE HAS TO HAVE THEIR HANDS ON IT FOR AN HOUR.

JENKINS' HANDS WERE MISSING, SO I THOUGHT THE KILLER HAD TAKEN THEM TO USE ON THE SAFE.

I THOUGHT ABOUT THAT, TOO.

OF COURSE YOU DID.

BUT...NO HANDS.

AND NO FINGERPRINTS, EITHER.

NOW THAT I THINK OF IT, DIDN'T THOMAS SAY IT HAD TO BE THE ENGINEER'S HANDS?

AND HE'S LOCKED IN THE ENGINE CAR. THERE'S NO WAY TO GET TO HIM.

SURE THERE IS...

...IF HE TRUSTS YOU ENOUGH TO OPEN THE DOOR AND LET YOU IN.

129

JESS' AX!

I'M THE ONLY ONE WHO CAN USE MY AX AND I HAVE AN ALIBI.

WHAT ABOUT THE ALASKAN KING CRAB BACK THERE? MAYBE HE SNIPPED IT OFF WITH HIS HUGE CLAW THINGS.

I DON'T THINK SO. THE CUT WAS FAR TOO CLEAN FOR THAT.

YOU ARE SO RIGHT! THE CHOICE OF A BLADE IS SO-O-O-O DAMNED IMPORTANT.

"IT'S GOTTA BE KEEN IF IT'S GONNA BE CLEAN!"

I LIKE THAT! I'M GONNA STEAL THAT!

A-HEM.

MAYBE SOMEONE USED THE TELEPORTATION ROD TO SEND HIS HEAD SOMEWHERE...BUT NOT HIS BODY.

WOULD THAT DO IT?

LISTEN!

I'M HAVING A MOMENT OF GENIUS AND I DON'T WANT TO WASTE IT!

JENKINS KILLED THE ENGINEER—

—HUDSON.

RIGHT.

JENKINS KILLED HUDSON HAWK AND TOOK THE HEAD SO THE BODY COULDN'T BE IDENTIFIED!

HE SWITCHED CLOTHES WITH HIM AND CHOPPED OFF HIS HANDS SO HE COULD USE THEM TO OPEN THE CRYPTSAFE!

HE'S AFTER OUR BOOTY!

NOT THE BOOTY!!

DRINK SERVICE!

WELL, YOU'RE OUT OF LUCK THERE, BUT I BET THERE'S A CAPRI SUN IN THE KITCHEN?

NO! THAT'S HOW JENKINS GOT TO THE ENGINEER! DURING DRINK SERVICE!

137

Chapter 6

145

YOU'RE GONNA LEVITATE HIM?

YEAH!

WE TIE A ROPE TO HIM. I LEVITATE HIM. HE HORIZONTALLY RAPPELS DOWN THE SIDE OF THE TRAIN TO THE CABOOSE DOOR!

LET ME MAKE ONE ADDENDUM TO YOUR PLAN HERE, TAAKO.

CAST LEVITATE SPECIFICALLY ON MY MAGIC JUMPING BOOTS.

THAT WAY I CAN KICK THEM OFF IF I NEED TO.

I LOVE IT! IT'S *DELECTABLE.* LET'S DO IT.

I GOTTA ADMIT, AT LEAST IT'LL BE FUN TO WATCH...

...AS YOU PING-PONG BACK AND FORTH BETWEEN THE TRAIN AND TUNNEL.

YOU STILL HORNY FOR IT?

AHEM.

THERE IS...

...LETTERMAN'S GAP.

HEIST PLANNING! I LOVE HEIST PLANNING!!

THE TRAIN WILL EMERGE FROM THIS SECTION OF THE TEETH AND CROSS OVER ON A SUSPENDED RAIL LINE BEFORE REENTERING THE MOUNTAINS.

AND THAT LAST TUNNEL GOES STRAIGHT TO EVERSUMMER.

LETTERMAN'S GAP IS THE ONLY TIME THE LIMITED WILL BE OUT IN THE OPEN BEFORE IT REACHES THE CITY.

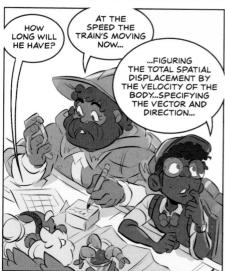

HOW LONG WILL HE HAVE?

AT THE SPEED THE TRAIN'S MOVING NOW...

...FIGURING THE TOTAL SPATIAL DISPLACEMENT BY THE VELOCITY OF THE BODY...SPECIFYING THE VECTOR AND DIRECTION...

...NINETY SECONDS?

IF WE'RE LUCKY.

SHIT. I REALLY WANTED TO BE CLOONEY, BUT I'M THE ACROBAT, AREN'T I?

YOU'RE THE ACROBAT.

POP!

...OF COURSE YOU'RE *SMART* ENOUGH TO REALIZE THAT THE ACROBAT IS THE MOST IMPORTANT PART OF THE PLAN...?

MAGNUS IS *SO* ON BOARD WITH THIS PLAN!!

149

EXCUSE ME, SIRS...

MAY I JUST SAY, SIRS, HOW VERY PROUD I AM OF YOU?

YOU'VE BEEN *MUCH* MORE COMPETENT THAN *ANYBODY* WOULD HAVE *EVER* THOUGHT!

WELL, THANK YOU, LITTLE GUY.

THAT'S VERY NICE OF YOU!

BUT YOU SHOULD WAIT 'TIL YOU GET TO KNOW US.

YEAH, WE BLEW UP A WHOLE CITY A FEW DAYS AGO.

SHRUG!

166

Chapter 7

THIS PLACE IS A *MESS*. IF JENKINS WAS STILL ALIVE I'D GROUND HIM FOR A WEEK!

WHATEVER, LET'S JUST FIND THE DEADLY MAGICAL ARTIFACT IN THIS PILE OF JUNK SO WE CAN GET THE HELL OUTTA HERE.

WHAT'S THE RUSH? I BET WE'VE GOT PLENTY OF TIME.

ACTUALLY, THE TRAIN WILL HIT EVERSUMMER IN SEVEN MINUTES...

...AND I DO MEAN *HIT.*

EVERYONE *STOP!*

AS YOU SIRS HAVE NO DOUBT SURMISED, JENKINS WAS THE ROCKPORT SLAYER.

WELL, OF *COURSE.*

THE SLAYER ALWAYS STOLE HIS VICTIMS' *MOST VALUABLE* POSSESSION.

JENKINS MUST HAVE HAD SOMETHING THAT SHOWED WHAT THE MOST VALUABLE ITEM WAS.

WELL THEN, TAAKO... YOU'D BETTER GRAB IT.

ME?

YOU RESISTED THE THRALL ON THE GAUNTLET! I BET YOU CAN DO IT AGAIN!

YEAH! WE BELIEVE IN YOU... CHAMP!

FWIP

FWIP

FWIP

FINE...

YOU BUNCHA BABIES.

CATCH!

KHHK

MAGNUS... COME IN MAGNUS.

HEY! WE GOT BARS!!

KILLIAN! YOU WON'T BELIEVE THIS!! I'M HAVING THE COOLEST TIME!!

I SOLVED A MURDER AND GOT TO MEET JESS THE BEHEADER AND THERE WAS THIS GIANT-ASS CRAB—

I'M SORRY, MAGNUS CAN'T COME TO THE STONE RIGHT NOW BECAUSE HE'S STARING IMMINENT DEATH AND MASSIVE DESTRUCTION IN THE FACE!!!!

HE'LL GET BACK TO YOU!

...MAYBE.

CRAB!

FLIP

SNAP!

WE HAVE TO GET INTO THE ENGINEER'S CAR AND STOP IT *NOW!!*

AS USUAL, IT'S UP TO ME TO SAVE THE DAMNED DAY!

...BY USING A POWERFUL MAGICAL ITEM I KNOW NOTHING ABOUT.

179

ARE YOU *SHITTING* ME? I'M TAAKO, BABY! TAAAAKO!

SLAYER OF SPIDERS! CHARMER OF BUGBEARS! FREEZER OF MEAT MONSTERS!!

TRUST ME!

...

JINGLE!

IS THIS FAKE CONFIDENCE YOUR ATTEMPT TO PROTECT ME BY GETTING ME TO JUMP...?

HEY, LOOK AT THAT! YOU FINALLY SOLVED A MYSTERY.

...OR TO DISTRACT ME FROM THAT BAG OF STUFF YOU TOOK FROM THE SAFE?

YOU KNOW WHAT?

FUCK IT!

I DO TRUST YOU!

VISIT GOLD

ME TOO...

I JUST CAN'T REACH ANY HIGHER.

...YOU *CAN* DO THIS, RIGHT?

MAN, I DON'T KNOW...

OUR TRACK RECORD WITH HEROIC DEEDS IS PRETTY LOUSY.

NO NO NO NO. YOU'RE APPROACHING IT ALL WRONG.

DON'T THINK OF THIS AS PRESERVING PROPERTY AND SAVING A BUNCH OF LIVES...

...THINK OF IT AS USING THAT TELEPORT ROD TO REALLY FUCK SOME PLACE UP WITH A TRAIN.

...*THAT,* I CAN DO.

Chapter 8

THE STATIONMASTER ASKED ME TO WRITE UP A REPORT ON EVERYTHING THAT HAPPENED!

I TELL YA, I THINK THIS JUST MIGHT BE MY FOOT IN THE DOOR TO GET A JOB WITH THE ROCKPORT LINE!

ONE SUGGESTION, GRAHAM:

YOU MIGHT NOT WANT TO PUT *EVERYTHING* IN YOUR LITTLE DISSERTATION. MAYBE OMIT THE WHOLE "DESTROYING THE TRAIN" PART.

MIGHT CAST...YOU...IN A BAD LIGHT.

SNIFF!

WOW, YOU GUYS...! ALWAYS THINKING OF OTHERS!

...I'LL NEVER FORGET YOU!

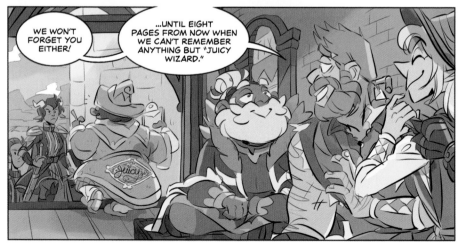

WE WON'T FORGET YOU EITHER!

...UNTIL EIGHT PAGES FROM NOW WHEN WE CAN'T REMEMBER ANYTHING BUT "JUICY WIZARD."

HEY! YOU THREE!

ARTEMIS STERLING, LORD OF EVERSUMMER, HAS QUESTIONS FOR YOU!

AHEM.

WHAT—

IT'S ALL RIGHT, SIR...

...THEY'RE WITH ME.

LORD ARTEMIS STERLING
Race Human
Class Royalty-Type Guy
→ PROFICIENCIES ←
→ Ruling
→ Administrating
→ Having an awesome name

...SEEMS LIKE A LOT OF AUTHORITY TO GIVE TO A KID...

WE DID IT, SIRS! WE SOLVED THE CASE.

THEN WHY DON'T YOU LOOK HAPPY, SHORT-PANTS?

I'M JUST KIND OF SAD BECAUSE I WAS TRANSPORTING MY GRANDPA'S FAVORITE SILVERWARE HOME FROM THE CLEANERS.

I DIDN'T THINK TO GRAB IT FROM THE CRYPTSAFE.

HE TOLD ME "I'D LIKE TO SEE THAT SILVERWARE ONE MORE TIME BEFORE I DIE...!"

FUNNY YOU SHOULD MENTION THAT...

YOU SAID...

...''GRAND RELICS...''?

THAT'S RIGHT...

THE GRAND RELICS ARE POWERFUL WEAPONS CREATED BY THE... RED ROBES.

A BAND OF WIZARDS, WARLOCKS, AND OTHER MAGIC USERS WHO WERE CARELESS WITH THEIR...MAGICAL EXPERIMENTATIONS.

THE RESULT OF THOSE EXPERIMENTS WAS THE CREATION OF WHAT WE CALL THE SEVEN GRAND RELICS.

THE BUREAU'S PURPOSE— MY PURPOSE— IS DESTROYING THEM.

FIVE.

WE'VE BROUGHT YOU...TWO RELICS.

...THAT LEAVES... FIVE, RIGHT?

YOU'RE RIGHT. FIVE.

FIVE RELICS REMAIN, AND THE RED ROBES WILL DO ANYTHING TO WIN THEM BACK.

MPLAINTS (LUCAS)

HOLD UP.

SO YOU'RE TELLING US THAT YOU AND YOUR BIG ORGANIZATION AND SECRET MOON BASE AND FLYING SNOW GLOBES, HAVE BEEN DOING THIS FOR HOWEVER LONG...

AND YOUR SCORE IS *ZERO*?!

TWO?

NO! THAT'S *OUR* SCORE!

YOU, ME, AND BEEFCAKE O'BURLY OVER THERE!

BOB INCORPORATED HAS A BIG OLD GOOSE EGG!

WHAT *EXACTLY* IS YOUR POINT, TAAKO?

MY POINT IS: I ONLY SIGNED UP FOR THIS GIG BECAUSE I THOUGHT YOU *KNEW* WHAT YOU WERE *DOING!*

YOU OWE US SOME *ANSWERS!*

WAIT!

WHERE DID YOU FIND THAT UMBRELLA?

THIS?

I FOUND IT LIKE TWO ADVENTURES AGO!

ON SOME SKELETON IN A CAVE.

SEE? ANSWERING SOMEONE'S QUESTION ISN'T HARD AT ALL...

...IS IT?

HOME, MICROSCOPIC HOME.

I'M NOT EVEN GONNA USE MY C-PAP SPELL TONIGHT.

AWWW, LOOK HOW SWEET!

THEY'RE SO CUTE WHEN THEY'RE ASLEEP.

I'M NOT... ASLEEP. I'M TOO...PISSED OFF... TO SLEEP...

WHAT ARE YOU PISSED OFF ABOUT, BUD?

WHY AREN'T THEY...MAKING...A FUSS...ABOUT US?

PROFESSIONAL JEALOUSY, MAYBE? THEY WISH THEY WERE COOL LIKE US?

IT TAKES TIME FOR PEOPLE TO ACCEPT THAT THEY'RE NO LONGER NEEDED.

YOU WATCH, BY THIS TIME NEXT WEEK THEY'LL BE TRYING TO PROMOTE US INTO MIDDLE MANAGEMENT.

BUT WE'LL BLOW 'EM OFF BECAUSE WE'RE TOO UNPREDICTABLE TO BE STUCK BEHIND A DESK.

OUR PLACE IS IN THE FIEL—

ZZZZZZ

ZZZZ

Fan Art Gallery

The Adventure Zone has been lucky enough to garner a passionate and deeply creative fandom. Many thanks to the fan artists who contributed pieces to this gallery—and to all the writers, artists, creators, and fans of all stripes who have made The Adventure Zone what it is. ♡

The ADVENTURE CONTINUES in

THE ADVENTURE ZONE

Petals to the Metal

Coming Soon!

Jay Pirfano

My Murphy

Gene McKechnie

Jeinu

Star Prichard

Pola Kowalewska

Sara Cliclicman

Glowbat

Phoebe Ayscough

EVERSUMMER

JESS

Karoline Stjernfelt

Devon Pasternak